The Third-Year Violoncello Method

by

A.W. BENOY
and
L. BURROWES

NOVELLO PUBLISHING LIMITED

Order No: NOV 916111

The Third-Year Cello Method

Order No: NOV 916111

10 lessons covering harmonics on A & D strings, tenor clef, fifth position, sixth position, seventh position, thumb position and treble clef, and higher positions.

ALSO AVAILABLE SEPARATELY

The First-Year Cello Method

Order No: NOV 915905

15 lessons covering open strings and first finger notes, first and second finger notes on D & A strings, bowing on successive open strings, first and third finger notes on G, D & A strings, bowing with two notes to the bow, and scales of G, D & C major.

The Second-Year Cello Method

Order No: NOV 915969

12 lessons covering crossing strings in key of C major, fourth position in keys of G & C major, half position, first finger extensions backwards in keys of B♭ & F major, forward finger extensions in keys of A & D major, second position, and third position.

Note: To save awkward turnovers, some of the early pieces have had to be contracted by means of Da Capo and Coda signs.

Lesson 1

Harmonic A and D

VIOLONCELLO CONCERTO

HAYDN

16111

Lesson 2
Tenor Clef

STUCK IM VOLKSTON

SCHUMANN
Op.102, No.1

Lesson 3
Fifth Position

EXERCISE

EASTER ALLELUYA

With dignity

STAINES MORRIS

Gaily

QUARTET, No 2

BORODIN

Lesson 4
Sixth Position

SARABANDE

HANDEL

16111

Lesson 5
Sixth Position

22

23 SCALE OF B♭ MAJOR

GO FROM MY WINDOW

Anon

24 Moderato

AFTON WATER

Traditional

Andante con moto

25
I
II

D string

LADY FRANCIS NEVILLE'S DELIGHT

Traditional

PLAISIR D'AMOUR

G. B. MARTINI

Andante tranquillo

27

16111

Lesson 6
Seventh Position

28

SCALE OF C MAJOR

29

ARPEGGIO OF C MAJOR

30

CAROL TUNE

Con moto

31

mf

dim.

OLD FRENCH MELODY

TCHAIKOWSKY
Op. 39, No. 16

Andante

32
I
II

p pizz

7th position

arco

ARIOSO

BACH

Lesson 7
Seventh Position

34

ARPEGGIO OF THE DOMINANT SEVENTH, F MAJOR

35

GIGUE

36

AUSTRIAN LÄNDLER

Traditional

37

MELODY

RUBINSTEIN

Lesson 8
Thumb Position and Treble Clef

39

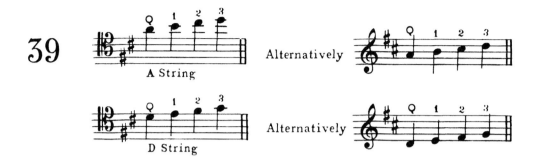

A String   Alternatively

D String   Alternatively

EASTER ALLELUYAH

40

THE THREE MARYS

Scottish Song

41

Andante

MARCH

BACH

Allegro

42

I

II

IRISH FOLK MELODY

Traditional

43

Lesson 9
Thumb Position

44

MILITARY SYMPHONY

HAYDN

45

CALLINO CASTUREME

Anon

46

47 SONATA IN G MINOR

ECCLES

TWENTY ONE EXERCISES FOR VIOLONCELLO, № 15

J.L. DUPORT

Lesson 10
Higher Positions

SCALE OF A MAJOR

GERMAN FOLK SONG

VITO

D. POPPER
Op. 54, N.º 5

51

STUDY

J.J.F. DOTZAUER

52